# Hiring
# an Employee

# Pocket Mentor Series

The *Pocket Mentor* Series offers immediate solutions to common challenges managers face on the job every day. Each book in the series is packed with handy tools, self-tests, and real-life examples to help you identify your strengths and weaknesses and hone critical skills. Whether you're at your desk, in a meeting, or on the road, these portable guides enable you to tackle the daily demands of your work with greater speed, savvy, and effectiveness.

**Books in the series:**

# Hiring an Employee

## Expert Solutions to Everyday Challenges

**Harvard Business Press**

Boston, Massachusetts

No part of this publication may be reproduced, stored in or introduced into a retrieval system, or transmitted, in any form, or by any means (electronic, mechanical, photocopying, recording, or otherwise), without the prior permission of the publisher. Requests for permission should be directed to permissions@hbsp.harvard.edu, or mailed to Permissions, Harvard Business School Publishing, 60 Harvard Way, Boston, Massachusetts 02163.

**Library of Congress Cataloging-in-Publication Data**

Hiring an employee : expert solutions to everyday challenges.
    p. cm. — (Pocket mentor series)
  Includes bibliographical references.
  ISBN 978-1-4221-2582-3
  1. Employees—Recruiting. 2. Employee selection. 3. Personnel management.
I. Harvard Business Press.
  HF5549.5.R44H557 2008
  658.3'11—dc22

                                      2008024629

The paper used in this publication meets the requirements of the American National Standard for Permanence of Paper for Publications and Documents in Libraries and Archives Z39.48-1992.

# Contents

# Mentor's Message: The Importance of Smart Hiring

Have you ever hired the wrong person? If so, you remember it well—and you probably recall the cost to both you and your group. Bad hiring decisions are both expensive and painful to correct.

By contrast, smart hiring choices can help you generate important value for your company—in the form of the workforce talent your organization needs to stay ahead of its competition. Your performance as a manager, as well as the performance of your group and entire firm, hinges tightly on your ability to make smart hiring decisions. Thus, the stakes are dauntingly high when you embark on the hiring process.

This book offers guidelines and tools for handling each step of the hiring process: defining job requirements, recruiting promising candidates, interviewing, evaluating the candidates you've interviewed, and finally, making a decision and then presenting a winning job offer.

Hiring right will always count among the most challenging tasks for any manager. But by using the ideas in this book, you'll sweeten the odds of building a powerful department or team that contributes directly to your company's—and your own—success.

## Linda A. Hill, Mentor

From her more than twenty years of extensive field work, professor Linda A. Hill has helped managers create the conditions for effective management in today's flatter and increasingly diverse organizations. She is a professor and chair of the Leadership Initiative at Harvard Business School. She is also the author of the best-selling *Becoming a Manager* (Harvard Business School Press), now available in paperback.

# Hiring an Employee: The Basics

# Understanding the Hiring Process

IRING GOOD PEOPLE is one of the most significant contributions you can make to your organization. Good hiring decisions create a foundation for effective performance by you, your team, and your company. Conversely, bad hiring decisions drag down performance and are expensive and painful to correct.

To ensure that you make the right hiring choices, it's helpful to begin with an overview of the hiring process.

## Five steps to effective hiring

Hiring involves careful thought about what the position you're filling entails, what characteristics are required to carry out its responsibilities successfully, and who would make a good candidate. You'll be more likely to hire the right person if you work closely with your human resource department during the entire hiring process. That process consists of the following five steps:

1. **Defining the job requirements.** Before you start the search, it's critical that you understand what the job involves and the education, skills, experience, and personal qualities that are needed to perform it.

2. **Recruiting promising candidates.** Once you know what the job requires, you need to find candidates who have the necessary

qualifications. The best way to find qualified candidates is to get the word out using your professional connections and recruiting resources.

3. **Interviewing.** You conduct interviews with the most promising candidates so you can learn more about their abilities and experience, as well as whether they will be a good fit with your organization. Interviews also provide you with an opportunity to "sell" the position and the company and give job candidates the information they need to make an informed decision.

4. **Evaluating the candidates.** Once all candidates have been interviewed, the people involved in the hiring decision must conduct an objective evaluation of each candidate.

5. **Making a decision and an offer.** The last step of the hiring process is making the decision and extending a job offer. During this step, you strive to always aim for the individual who can contribute the most to your organization's success.

Each of these steps helps you refine your candidate search. In the sections that follow, we'll examine each step in detail.

# Step 1: Defining Job Requirements

EFORE YOU CAN hire the right person for the job, you need to understand what the job involves. You also want to determine what will make for a good "fit" between an individual's skills and personal attributes and the requirements of the job and the organization. There are three factors that will help you define the job and its requirements:

- **Background characteristics**, such as education and past experience

- **Personal characteristics**, such as creative abilities and decision-making style

- **Organizational structure**, such as hierarchy and management, and culture, including values and accepted ways of interacting

To get a sense of the primary responsibilities and tasks that a particular role entails, begin by asking, "What does the employee have to do in this job?" If you are looking to fill an existing position, you can often answer this question by reviewing the current job description. If you are hiring for a newly created position or if a job description does not exist for the role, you will need to spend time learning about the job function and talking with those who will interact with or rely on the person who holds this position.

Let's take a closer look at the factors essential for defining job requirements.

## Identifying ideal background characteristics

When you think about a candidate's background, the two major factors to consider are education and experience. Determine whether a specific educational background is truly necessary for the job. Sometimes, you may find you can be flexible and substitute a certain educational background and degree with relevant experience.

Base the experience requirements on a thorough analysis of the specific tasks and responsibilities the position entails. Distinguish between the type and level of experience that are absolutely critical for the job and those that are beneficial but not essential. Determine whether the organization can afford the time needed for on-the-job learning for a strong candidate who lacks some of the experience requirements.

Also consider whether you want someone with industry experience, functional experience (such as expertise in marketing, finance, or customer service), and large- versus small-company experience. Note that industry and functional experience are particularly important for externally oriented positions requiring knowledge of products and competitors.

## Stipulating required personal qualities

Personal qualities indicate how the candidate will approach the job and interact with coworkers. Evaluate the following qualities

# What Would YOU Do?

## Torn Between Two Techies

FRANK IS FEELING plagued by indecision. He has to choose between two very qualified, yet very different, applicants for a high-level technician job at MotionTech. He has been leaning toward Jeanette, the slightly less experienced candidate, who has demonstrated a developing talent in certain skills over the past two years. And she comes from an informal culture similar to MotionTech's. But Frank's colleague, Mary, sees more potential in Chad, the other candidate. She's impressed by his record of high performance and likes the fact that some of his old teammates—also very skilled—might follow him to his new job. It doesn't bother Mary that Chad comes from a more structured culture. Frank wonders to himself, "Which are the *most* important attributes to look for in a candidate for this position?"

What would YOU do? The mentor will suggest a solution in *What You COULD Do*.

relative to the tasks and responsibilities you've listed for the job opening:

- **Analytical and creative abilities.** A candidate's abilities in these two areas determine how he or she assesses problems and comes up with new approaches to solving them. Does the job need a problem solver or someone who is comfortable working within established processes?

- **Decision-making style.** The way people make decisions is very individual. Some people are extremely analytical and rely on facts, while others rely more on intuition. Some make decisions quickly, while others ponder them for a long time. Some depend on consensus, while others seek their own counsel. It is critical to determine whether a particular decision-making style is required for success in the job and, if so, what that style is.

- **Interpersonal skills.** To determine which interpersonal skills are most appropriate for a given position, think about the set of tasks that will be performed in the position. Which characteristics (attitudes, values, and behaviors) would translate into good performance, especially in view of the superiors, peers, and direct reports with whom the person will interact? For example, an effective controller might be patient and formal, demonstrating careful, cautious, detail-oriented behavior. For a sales manager, high extroversion and informality might be desirable. For a person who will have to catalyze needed change (for example, designing new ways of carrying out a particular business process), a talent for winning others' buy-in could be essential.

- **Motivation.** A candidate's goals, interests, energy level, and job progression often demonstrate his or her level of motivation. If the position calls for a high degree of independence, you might look for goal-oriented, high-energy, or self-directed candidates.

*"If each of us hires people who are smaller than we are, we shall become a company of dwarfs. But if each of us hires people who are bigger than we are, we shall become a company of giants."*
—David Ogilvy

## Considering organizational structure and culture

In addition to thinking about candidate attributes that match the specific job requirements, you need to widen your perspective and consider how a candidate will fit in with the organization as a whole. Think about how your organization is structured, and try to determine what characteristics would be a good fit with the environment.

For example, is your organization hierarchical and formal or less structured and informal? Some candidates might not function well in an informal and less structured environment, while others may indicate that a limited structure fuels their creativity.

It's also important to think about the culture of your company. Culture defines an organization's way of doing things, general values, and the ways in which people relate to one another. The culture of an organization displays itself in factors such as how people dress, whether they restrict conversations to professional matters, or whether people tend to work in teams or independently. Think about the culture of your organization and how it might be described in terms of employee attributes.

In thinking about culture, also consider the "microculture" of your team or department. In some organizations, particular teams or departments might have a culture that differs from that of the overall company. If this is true about your own group, you'll want to look for job candidates who make a good match for the group's microculture.

## Developing a job description

Once you understand the position's requirements, you are ready to create a job description. A job description outlines the job responsibilities, reporting relationships, hours, compensation, and credentials needed. It will allow you to explain the job both to potential candidates and to any resources (such as a search firm) you might be using to help you identify candidates. In some cases, your organization may have a required format or standard job description to use as a model, and you may need to have certain aspects of the description, such as salary, approved by the human resource department. Your job description should include the following information:

- Job title, business unit, organization
- Summary of the job tasks, responsibilities, and objectives
- Hiring manager, reporting manager
- Compensation, hours, location
- Background (education, experience) required
- Personal characteristics required

Remember, creating a job description is also an opportunity to redesign a job, not just to fill the current one. For example, the last person who held the position might have had a strong strategic focus, and you may decide you now need a more hands-on manager. Develop the job description accordingly. And don't forget to ask for insights from the people who will have to work with the new hire. That way, you can ensure that you've accurately described the job in terms of roles and responsibilities within your team. The table "Sample job description for a senior accountant," on page 16, shows one example of a well-written job description.

# What You COULD Do.

Remember Frank's worries about which attributes he should emphasize in evaluating candidates for the technician job?

Here's what the mentor suggests:

One tool that Frank might use to compare Jeanette and Chad is a decision-making matrix. (You'll learn more about this tool later in the book.) To create a decision-making matrix, he should list the candidates along one side of the grid and the job requirements across the top. Frank should then decide on a scoring system to use to rank each candidate's fit with the job requirements. The next step is to fill in the matrix using the notes he took during the interviews. After that, Frank should check each candidate's references. If the decision on whom to hire is not clear by the end of this process, Frank might want to schedule second interviews with the two candidates.

Frank should also examine his own thinking to make sure he hasn't fallen victim to common biases in hiring—such as seeing higher potential in people who are similar to ourselves. And he can recall his observations of the two candidates' behaviors, to see whether any particular behaviors shed light on each person's possible fit with the company. For instance, if he had lunch with each candidate at a local restaurant, how did the interviewee treat the waiter? Aloofness or lack of respect may speak volumes about how the person will treat others once he or she starts the new job.

## Sample job description for a senior accountant

**Date:**            October 1, 2008
**Position title:**    Senior accountant
**Hours/location:**   Monday–Friday, 9:00–5:00; Watertown office
**Compensation:**   $70,000–$75,000 annual salary
**Department:**     Finance
**Reports to:**      Assistant director, finance
**Works with:**      Inventory manager, accounts payable and receivable staff

**Summary:** (summary statement/brief overview of position)

As a member of the accounting team, support the management of the company through timely and accurate reporting of financial information and analysis of our inventory position.

**Key responsibilities:** (specific key duties/responsibilities of position)

- Contribute to an accurate and speedy close through completion of account reconciliations and other actions as required.
- Liaise with product business groups and partner-distributors to analyze operational information and create worksheets used to post journal entries to the general ledger.
- Ensure accurate transfer of data from the perpetual inventory system to the general ledger, determine that the system is functioning properly, and recommend system improvements. Implement cycle count procedures during cycle counts to determine correctness and recommend improvements.
- Assist with licensing processing as required.
- Liaise between outside distributors and internal departments for sales data, and perform analysis of data to ensure accurate and reliable information.
- Reconcile selected accounts to the appropriate subsidiary ledgers, and perform account analysis to ensure appropriate adjustments are recorded.
- Prepare segments of the annual audit work paper package as assigned, in an accurate and timely manner.
- Special projects as assigned.

**Requirements:** (education, experience, communication/organization skills, work environment, etc.)

- College degree, preferably in accounting or business administration.
- Two to three years of progressive responsibility in general accounting.
- Excellent interpersonal skills as well as the ability to communicate well both verbally and in writing.

# Step 2: Recruiting Promising Candidates

ACCESSING QUALIFIED candidates is critical to the success of your hiring effort. You can recruit the most promising candidates by using the right recruitment channels and carefully screening the résumés you receive.

## Using the right recruitment channels

You will want to get the word out about the open position through as many channels as possible to increase the number of applicants in your candidate pool. Certainly you should use your own network of contacts to look for potential new hires. These contacts may include former colleagues who have moved to another company and members of clubs or other social organizations you belong to. However, don't rely solely on your network, as it may not give you access to diverse candidates. For this reason, you should also select additional targeted, relevant channels to ensure that the proportion and diversity of qualified candidates in your pool is as high as possible. Typical channels include:

- Recruiting agencies
- Newspaper ads
- Referrals from colleagues

- Trade publications
- Professional associations
- Networking
- Colleges and universities
- The Internet (recruitment Web sites and your company's Web site)
- Job fairs

Signaling inclusivity when you communicate your policies, benefits, and mission statements can help ensure a diverse candidate pool. In addition, you can enhance the candidate "pipeline" through programs like internships and partnerships with colleges, universities, and community organizations. You can also take advantage of your company's college recruitment programs as well as encourage personal referrals from current employees.

In reviewing potential recruitment channels, always consider internal as well as external candidates. If you never hire from within, you won't be able to develop an organizational culture that attracts talented people seeking a promising future within your firm. But be aware: we tend to fall victim to a certain cognitive bias when considering other people's merits. People we're already familiar with (for example, employees we know from our own company) can sometimes look more flawed than individuals we haven't met yet (external candidates). Keep this in mind as you analyze the pros and cons of potential candidates from inside and outside your company.

> **Tip:** When recruiting to fill an open or new position, don't forget to consider current employees in your department or in other departments in the organization. Current employees will probably already make a good cultural match and will be familiar with the company's values and ways of working.

## Screening résumés

The cover letter and résumé a candidate sends to your company is that person's first introduction to you. These documents' contents should convey the qualities you are looking for. Note that e-mailed submissions may be less formal than traditionally mailed résumés or provided in a format specific to an online recruiting agency.

When you have a large number of résumés to review, use a two-step process to make your task more manageable. In the first pass, eliminate the résumés for those candidates who clearly do not meet the education and experience requirements that you previously noted as being essential for performing the job. Examine specific aspects of the résumé, such as:

- Signs of achievement and results; for example, profit orientation, stability, or career direction

- Progressive career momentum

- A career goal in line with the job being offered

- Willingness to work hard

- Overall construction and appearance of the résumé, although this criterion may not apply to résumés submitted via an online form

In the second pass, consider the more subtle differences among qualified candidates. For example, perhaps one person has slightly more experience or education required for the job than another. Then develop a list of the strongest candidates.

---

**Tip:** Spend the smallest amount of your time on eliminating the least likely candidates and the greatest amount of your time carefully considering the most likely candidates.

---

When reviewing résumés, also be on the alert for warning signs that can indicate areas of weakness, such as:

- Lengthy description of education (possibly not much job experience)

- Obvious gaps in background

- Too much personal information (possibly not much job experience)

- Descriptions of jobs and positions only, with no descriptions of results or accomplishments

- Typographical errors and poor reproduction quality (signaling carelessness or sloppiness)

## Steps for Recruiting Candidates

1. **Define job requirements.** A clear definition of the job requirements will help you determine what will make for a good fit between an individual's skills and personal attributes and the needs of the job and the organization.

2. **Develop a job description.** A job description allows you to explain the job both to potential candidates and to resources you may be using to help you identify candidates. Keep in mind that this is an opportunity to redesign a job, not simply to fill the current position.

3. **Get the word out.** You will want to get the word out through as many relevant channels as possible to maximize the number of qualified applicants in your candidate pool.

4. **Screen résumés.** When you have a large number of résumés to review, use a two-step process to make your task more manageable. In the *first pass*, eliminate the résumés for those candidates who do not meet the basic requirements of the job. In the *second pass*, consider the more subtle differences among qualified candidates. Then develop a list of the strongest candidates. Be on the alert for *red flags* that can signal weakness in a résumé.

# Step 3: Interviewing Candidates

INTERVIEWING JOB candidates is the heart of the hiring process, and many managers find this step particularly complex and challenging. In the sections below, we'll explore keys to tackling this challenge: understanding the interviewing process, choosing an interview approach, preparing for the interview, conducting the interview, maintaining control of the interview, and asking the right questions.

## Understanding the interviewing process

A hiring interview has one primary purpose: to provide an opportunity for both interviewer and job candidate to obtain the information they need to make the best possible decision. Since the time spent with any particular job candidate is limited, a well-organized approach will help make the most of that time, yielding more and better information.

To interview someone for an important position, you may go through all of the following stages. You'll probably go through at least two to three of them for every job opening.

1. **Create an interview team.** Before you begin interviewing candidates, you may want to set up an interview team to help with the process. The interview team should comprise a select few people who are familiar with the job function, who will be interacting with the person who is ultimately hired, and who

may be present during the actual job interviews. The team may include a representative from the human resource function, other managers, peers, and direct reports. Each team member brings different experience and perspective to the process, resulting in a broader view that is more likely to lead to a successful hiring decision.

If you've decided to have multiple people present during each job interview, you may want to assign each person to cover a specific set of questions with the candidate. That way, you stand a better chance of ensuring that all the important topics are covered during each interview.

2. **Telephone-screening interview.** You or someone from a recruiting agency, the interview team, HR, or your department may conduct a telephone-screening interview. The purpose of this phone call is to confirm that the candidate meets the stated job qualifications. It is also a good opportunity to get some initial impressions of the candidate: Does he or she call you back at the specified time? Communicate well? Sound confident and motivated?

3. **Initial in-person interview.** Try to narrow the field to four to seven candidates before holding an initial interview. This interview will probably last thirty to sixty minutes. For less demanding positions, you may find out everything you need to know about the candidate in this initial in-person interview. In other cases, you will need to see the person again.

4. **Second interview.** Be very selective about which candidates are asked back for a second interview. At this point, if you

don't have an interview team, you might ask others with a stake in the process to meet the candidate. These may include direct reports, potential peers, or other managers. This interview often brings out more of the "real" person.

5. **Final interview.** Schedule a final interview with each candidate during which time you and, if appropriate, your manager "sell" the job and the organization to the candidates. You may also want the candidates to meet with someone from HR to learn briefly about company policies and benefits.

## Choosing an interview approach

The approach you use when interviewing may vary with the type of position you are trying to fill and your comfort level with the interview process. Two basic approaches are structured and unstructured interviews.

In a *structured interview*, you ask all of the candidates the same questions so you can compare answers. The purpose of structured interviews is to be fair and objective. However, this approach may not elicit as much information from candidates as unstructured interviews. Structured interviews are more appropriate for positions that don't require much judgment or creative thinking.

*Unstructured interviews* are individual conversations that do not necessarily cover all the same questions with every candidate. You may learn more about each candidate, but it will be difficult to compare their responses. This type of interview is beneficial when you are filling a position that involves a fair amount of decision making, problem solving, and interaction with others. It opens the door to productive areas of inquiry that neither you nor your colleagues may have anticipated.

In most cases, it's probably a good idea to steer a middle path between these two interview approaches. Be flexible in your line of inquiry, but be sure that all interviewees respond to a core set of questions. By preparing those core questions in advance, you can assure yourself and the decision-making team that all key points are covered and that all candidates respond to them.

## Preparing for the interview

To prepare for an interview, it's helpful to develop an interview guide. This guide helps you be consistent, focused, and fair in your interviews. It also helps you maintain control of the interview—ensuring that you extract the information you need from the candidate. You can develop one general interview guide per job opening and then create individualized copies that contain each candidate's information. During the interview, you can use the customized guide as a road map and as a place to take notes.

An interview guide contains the following information:

- A summary of the job requirements as outlined in your job description

- The candidate's relevant experience and accomplishments

- Questions to ask to determine whether the candidate has the qualities you want; some questions should be general and asked of all candidates, while other questions should be customized for each candidate

The table "Example interview guide" shows questions to explore specific information in a job candidate's résumé.

In preparing your guide, think of ways to look beyond job titles on a candidate's résumé. Craft questions that will encourage the person to talk about what he or she actually did in that previous role, who he or she worked with, and so forth. You want to find out the day-to-day realities of the person's previous position, including the challenges he or she faced and how the individual handled those challenges. For example, to whom did the person go for help on what types of challenges? The candidate's responses to such questions will tell you a lot about how he or she might behave in the new role.

## Example interview guide

| If the résumé states: | Ask: |
| --- | --- |
| "I successfully managed development of a new line of consumer kitchenware." | "How was success measured: by revenues, time-to-market, or some other criteria? Specifically, what was your role in the development effort?" |
| "I worked effectively with marketing and sales to increase annual unit sales by 25% over the past 12 months." | "What was the nature of your contribution? How were unit sales increased: by more effective selling or by reducing prices?" |
| "I initiated the redesign of key department processes." | "What processes? What do you mean by 'initiated'? Why did you decide to do this? Why was this initiative important?" |

Before you distribute interview guides to the interview team, it's always prudent to have your human resource department and/or legal counsel review these guides to ensure that they do not include any questions that you may not legally ask. (See the section "Asking the right questions" for more information on this.)

In addition, remember that you will be able to gather more of the information you need to make a good hiring decision if you take the time and trouble to prepare carefully for interviews. Equally important, you'll leave a better impression on the candidate if you are organized and efficient. This is important because the candidate is interviewing you and your company, too.

To further prepare for an interview:

- Read the candidate's résumé and cover letter.

- Find out where the candidate is in the interviewing process, with whom they have previously interviewed, and what additional information he or she may have provided in previous interviews.

- Become familiar with the job function.

- Review the questions in your interview guide.

- Know what your organization has to offer candidates and what the candidate is looking for so that you can promote your organization and the job opportunity.

- Be up to date on your organization's reputation.

- Practice your interviewing skills by role-playing with a colleague.

## Conducting the interview

There are three phases to the interview: the opening, body, and close.

The *interview opening* should constitute about 10 percent of the allotted time for the interview. Your goal during the opening is to make the candidate feel comfortable and to set expectations about the structure of the interview. There are several things you can do to set the right tone at the beginning of the interview. For example:

- **Greet the candidate.** To put the candidate at ease, be warm and friendly. Introduce yourself. Smile, make eye contact, and shake hands. Include the candidate's name in your greeting. If you are not sure how to pronounce it, ask. Be aware of cultural nuances. For instance, if the candidate makes a small bow during the greeting, do so yourself to show respect.

- **Select a quiet, private meeting space that will not be conducive to interruptions.** Activate your voice mail or redirect your phone calls; do not take any calls or visitors during the interview.

- **Make sure the candidate is physically comfortable.** In the interview space, show the candidate where to put his or her coat and where to sit. Offer the candidate a beverage.

- **Introduce yourself.** Explain your role in the organization and how it relates to the open position.

- **Explain the structure of the interview.** For example, you might say: "I'm going to ask you about your experience." "I'm interested in finding out about you as an individual." "We're interested in learning whether there is a good fit between your interests and abilities and our organization's needs." "I will tell you about our organization." "I'll be glad to take your questions at the end of the interview."

- **Establish rapport with the candidate.** There are several approaches you can use. For instance, acknowledge some of the difficulties or awkwardness related to being interviewed, such as meeting a lot of new people or being tired at the end of the day. If you are the first to interview the candidate, ask how his or her commute was or whether the person had any difficulty finding your building. Compliment the candidate on some aspect of the experience displayed in his or her résumé. Acknowledge that you have something in common, such as attending the same college or sharing an outside interest.

The *interview body* should take up about 80 percent of the allotted time. During this phase, you gather the information you will need to evaluate the candidate. You want to assess the candidate's qualifications, skills, knowledge, and experience and compare them with the job description you created. Pursue a direct line of questions based on the person's résumé. Identify similarities and patterns of behavior consistent with your ideal candidate. If appropriate, ask for samples of work, transcripts, and references to review after the interview.

It can sometimes be difficult to get the candidate to be specific about accomplishments listed on his or her résumé. Ask directly for details, and probe for tangible measures of success. And be sure to pose the questions you listed while preparing the interview guide. For example, if the résumé states, "I played the leading role in the best-rated show," ask, "How was the success of your performance measured? Specifically, what was your role in achieving the show's ratings?"

During the body of the interview, you are also assessing the candidate's personal qualities, such as leadership or decision-making style, problem-solving approach, communication skills, teamwork skills, and motivation. Ask behavioral and scenario-based questions about past experiences and what-if situations. For example, "What was your biggest challenge in your previous job, and how did you address it?" "What would you do if sales began dropping suddenly six months after you started in this job?" Look for an understanding of the job, enthusiasm, a willingness to learn, and potential fit in the organization and in your team or department.

You also "sell" your organization during this part of the interview, by explaining what's special about your company's culture or its standing in the industry and by pointing out potential developmental opportunities (such as fast-track career paths) that the candidate might consider important. Be careful, though, that you don't make promises you can't keep. For example, suppose you overstate the speed of career advancement in your company to win a talented, high-potential recruit. Once the person is on board and discovers the truth (that career advancement takes place more slowly than you said), he or she may jump ship to a rival company that offers more attractive opportunities.

During the interview body, also make sure you don't prematurely discriminate against the candidate by misinterpreting the person's behavior. For example, many women need more time than men to tout their own skills and expertise during a job interview. If you don't allow a female candidate that time, you may mistakenly conclude that she's not right for the job.

Management professors Debra Meyerson and Joyce Fletcher wrote about this in their April 2002 *Harvard Business Review* article, "A Modest Manifesto for Shattering the Glass Ceiling":

> *A major investment firm provides another example of how invisible—even unintentional—gender discrimination thrives in today's companies. The firm sincerely wanted to increase the number of women it was hiring from business schools. It reasoned it would be able to hire more women if it screened more women, so it increased the number of women interviewed during recruiting visits to business school campuses. The change, however, had no impact. Why? Because, the 30 minutes allotted for each interview—the standard practice at most business schools—was not long enough for middle-aged male managers, who were conducting the vast majority of the interviews, to connect with young female candidates sufficiently to see beyond their directly relevant technical abilities. Therefore, most women were disqualified from the running. They hadn't had enough time to impress their interviewer.*

The *interview close* should occupy about 10 percent of the allotted time for the interview. During this phase, you answer any

Step 3: Interviewing Candidates    **33**

remaining questions the candidate may have, explain the next steps in the hiring process, and thank the candidate for coming. The table "Wrapping up the interview" outlines what the close entails.

Some candidates may ask questions about salary or benefits at this stage. In some organizations, the human resource department

## Wrapping up the interview

| What to do: | What to say: |
|---|---|
| Ask whether the candidate has anything else to add. | "Is there anything else you wanted to tell me about that I did not give you a chance to discuss?" |
| Ask whether the candidate has questions or whether there is anything that hasn't been covered or that is unclear. | "I see our time is almost up. Before we close, is there a question or two I might be able to answer for you?" |
| Explain how and when the candidate will hear about follow-up interviews or a decision. | "We will review all of the information and be in touch with you by (date)." |
| Give the candidate your business card. Invite him or her to call you with further questions. | "Here's my card. Please feel free to contact me if you have any other questions." |
| Promote your organization. Remember to target the features of your organization that would appeal to the candidate. | "I hope you'll strongly consider our organization. As the leader in the field, we have many fascinating projects in the pipeline and many more in our future." |
| Thank the applicant. Shake hands and make eye contact. Walk the candidate to the door or to his or her next destination. | "Thank you for your time and for helping us learn more about your experience. I believe you are meeting with Stan next. Let me walk you to his office." |

addresses these questions. However, you may need to address them yourself. Be prepared. If you don't have the information, tell the candidate you will get it to him or her when you have it.

*"It's not about you [the manager]; it's about your team and the success of your team. [And] one of the most important skills is hiring."*
—Aart de Geus

## Maintaining control of the interview

The goal of a job interview is to learn as much as possible about the candidate. You therefore need to keep the conversation focused, encourage the candidate to talk, and take notes so that you remember important information about the individual.

The key to maintaining control is to ask most of the questions and do most of the listening. You should be listening 80 percent of the time. The following practices can help:

- Follow logical lines of inquiry, and return to them if the candidate asks a question.

- Avoid having the candidate ask questions until the end of the interview.

- If the candidate gets off track in answering a question, gently steer him or her back to your topic. Use phrases such as "You were saying earlier . . ." or "Tell me more about . . .".

- Actively listen. Focus on what the person is saying, and withhold judgment.

- Regularly summarize what you hear to confirm what has been said, to make transitions between topics, and to limit the comments of a wordy candidate. An example of such a summary would be, "Are you saying that there was a six-month period when you were supervising twenty people in two different departments? That must have been difficult. How did you stay organized and on top of what was happening?"

The more you can encourage the candidate to talk, the more accurate your picture of him or her will be. You can use the following active-listening techniques:

- Smile, nod, and leave pauses before you jump in with a comment or another question.

- Ask follow-up questions that lead to more elaboration and specific examples of key information about the candidate.

- Use the candidate's response in your follow-up questions.

- Use open-ended questions that incorporate terms such as *how*, *why*, *can you describe*, and *tell me about*.

---

**Tip:** While interviewing candidates, follow the 80/20 rule. Get the candidate to do 80 percent of the talking. The person asking questions and listening is the person who's in control of the interview.

---

Try to monitor your own reactions. Avoid reacting negatively to what the interviewee has to say—otherwise, he or she will not respond as candidly to future questions. Know your own biases, and try to control their influence. Your first impression may change as the interview progresses. Some people make a great impression in the first few minutes, yet become less impressive as they talk more. Other people are nervous or slow to warm up, and their strengths take longer to emerge.

---

Tip: During interviews, don't buy first impressions. You may miss the opportunity to get to know the real person.

---

Notes help you recall significant facts about the candidate. Do take notes, but be unobtrusive about it. Tell the candidate up front that you will be taking notes. Remember that your notes will become part of the employee file. Avoid writing anything down (such as the person's race) that could be construed as inconsistent with equal opportunity employment laws. Also, take time between interviews to write down any additional notes or observations while they are still fresh in your mind.

*"If you have both the support of your team and a clear line of sight as to what the [new hire] will do, the chances are much better that you will attract somebody great to your team."*
—Aart de Geus

## Asking the right questions

The job interview is all about asking effective questions that get your candidate to talk freely about him- or herself. An effective question meets the following criteria:

- Has a purpose.

- Generates information about the person's qualifications.

- Opens communication.

- Is job related.

- Is not "leading"; that is, it doesn't prompt the person to say what you'd like to hear him or her say. An example of a leading question might be, "Would you say you have the motivation required for this job?" A nonleading version of this question could be, "What interests you most about this job?"

- Is nonthreatening; it doesn't put the person on the defensive. An example of a threatening question might be, "Why did you let these manufacturing problems accumulate?" A nonthreatening version of this question could be, "What led to the increase in manufacturing problems that you've described?"

Effective questions reflect favorably on you and demonstrate your interest. The candidate will sense that you took time to develop thoughtful questions. Moreover, you are more likely to elicit the information you need to effectively evaluate the candidate if you vary the types of questions you use during the interview. The table "A menu of question types" lists the different types of questions you might ask.

## A menu of question types

| Question type | Example |
|---|---|
| **Open-ended questions** begin with *what*, *how*, *why*, *when*, or *where*. They invite long answers that encourage the candidate to do most of the talking. | "When were you a member of a team? Can you describe what it was like?" |
| **Closed questions** begin with *did*, *would*, *do*, and *are*. These questions can be answered yes or no. They should be used sparingly because they do not encourage the candidate to talk. | "Do you have any experience working on a team?" |
| **Self-appraisal questions** require the candidate to give some thought to his or her interpersonal skills and abilities. They allow the candidate, rather than you, to interpret the facts. | "Why do you think you were selected to lead the task force?" |
| **Accomplishment questions** provide evidence of the candidate's demonstrated behavioral qualities. They help you learn why and how something was accomplished. They also reveal a candidate's level of involvement in the accomplishment. | "Tell me about a contribution you have made to a team effort." |
| **Broad-brush questions** prompt the candidate to think about a big topic, choose an answer, and organize his or her thoughts. | "Tell me about your experience as a project manager with the fiber optics group." |
| **Comparison questions** reveal a candidate's analytical and reasoning abilities. | "How would you compare working with the fiber optics group to working with the polymer group?" |

In most cases, you'll want to ask about the candidate's most recent job, work experience, skills, working style, career aspirations, and education. The table "Questions about specific topics" provides some sample questions for each topic.

## Questions about specific topics

| Topic area | Sample questions |
|---|---|
| Introduction | • "How did you hear about this job opening?"<br>• "What attracted you to this organization?" |
| Most recent job | • "Describe a typical day in your current/most recent position."<br>• "What do you find most satisfying/frustrating about the job?"<br>• "What is the most challenging aspect of your position?"<br>• "What have you learned most from the job? How has that contributed to your growth?" |
| Work experience | • "How has your work experience prepared you for this job?"<br>• "Describe one or two of your greatest accomplishments and biggest disappointments."<br>• "What has been the most significant challenge you have managed? How did you manage it?" |
| Skills | • "What is your greatest strength that would benefit our organization?"<br>• "Describe a time when you worked to meet a customer's needs."<br>• "Tell me about a time you when you had to evaluate a situation to resolve a problem. What was the situation, and what actions did you take?" |
| Style | • "How have you preferred to be supervised in your previous jobs?"<br>• "What type of organization do you prefer to work for?"<br>• "What kinds of people do you like to work with?" |
| Career aspirations | • "How does this job fit into your overall career plans?"<br>• "Where do you see yourself three years from now?"<br>• "In what areas would you like to receive additional training if you got this job?" |
| Education | • "What courses have prepared you for this position?"<br>• "What got you interested in this field and your course of study?" |

Also, depending on the requirements of the position, you might ask questions that help you learn more about the candidate's personal qualities, such as adaptability, team effectiveness, self-control, or professional confidence.

During a job interview, you'll want to avoid asking illegal questions. In the United States, topics that are not legal to discuss in an interview include the candidate's:

- Age
- Religion
- Race
- Citizenship
- Physical attributes
- Sexual orientation
- National origin
- Marital status
- Children
- Day care arrangements
- Arrests
- Place of residence; whether the person owns or rents his or her place of residence
- Previous workers' compensation claims
- Disabilities/physical ailments
- Specific promise of salary expectations

U.S., federal, state, and local laws and regulations are clear about what questions are illegal. If you are not familiar with these laws and regulations, consult your human resource specialist or legal counsel.

Even if you can't ask certain questions legally during an interview, you can still get the information you need (for example, will the new hire be able to travel as needed in the job?) if you phrase the questions in a legal manner. The table "Getting the information you need" shows examples.

## Getting the information you need

| If you need to know . . . | Don't ask . . . | Do ask . . . |
| --- | --- | --- |
| Whether the candidate is eligible to work in the United States | "Are you a citizen of the United States?" | "If hired, can you show proof of your eligibility to work in the United States?" |
| Whether the person can travel and work long hours as needed in the job | "Do you have children that you need to take to day care?" or "What is your religion?" | "This position requires travel and work during some evenings. Would you be able to meet these requirements?" or "This job requires that you work weekends. Would you be able to meet this requirement?" |
| Whether the interviewee can perform the physical tasks required by the job | "Do you have any health-related issues that would prohibit you from doing this job?" | "This job requires that you lift 50 pounds. Are you able to meet this requirement?" |
| Whether the candidate is of legal age to work | "How old are you?" | "If hired, can you show proof that you are at least eighteen years of age?" |

# Step 4: Evaluating Candidates

ONCE YOU'VE INTERVIEWED a number of candidates, how do you determine which ones seem to be the most promising? The following sections can help you make that determination. Keys include using a decision-making matrix, avoiding common evaluation mistakes, and checking references carefully.

## Using a decision-making matrix

A decision-making matrix can be a useful tool for comparing the candidates you've interviewed. Because the matrix helps you establish a formal process, it can also introduce more rationality into the evaluation stage of hiring. And rationality is important for counteracting the cognitive biases (such as feeling more of an affinity for people who are similar to you) that can creep in during this stage.

To create a decision-making matrix, list your candidates along one side of a grid, and list your job requirements across the top. Decide on a scoring system that you will use to rank each candidate's fit with each of the job requirements. To fill in the matrix, use the notes you took during and between interviews as well as impressions you gained from your conversations with the candidates.

Keep the following data in mind as you create your evaluation:

- Personal characteristics

- Education/training

- Essential performance factors
- Compatibility with organizational culture and management style
- Compatibility with the organization's reward system
- Ability to grow with and within the organization
- Elimination factors
- Essential technical experience
- Overall assessment

In filling out your matrix, also consider the question of how much weight you want to give to candidates' potential and attitude versus how much for their past performance. Many companies that want to recruit talented people who can grow and develop as the organization changes will emphasize potential and attitude over past performance. Find out whether this is a major objective at your firm, and evaluate the candidates accordingly. Of course, a new hire must bring the skills needed to carry out the job. And he or she will need to fit into your team's and company's culture. But if you're looking for someone who will also be able to grow with your firm, keep an eye out for an attitude that says, "I want to take on new challenges; I want to learn."

Finally, in evaluating candidates, don't limit your thinking to just the current position. Also consider each person's aspirations and ability to learn, and how these might relate to your company's future needs. Specifically, how likely is it that a particular candidate will be interested in *and* able to develop new skills (such as innovation, process improvement, and customer intimacy) that will be essential for your firm to stay competitive in the coming years? In other words, take a long-term view of each candidate's potential.

> Tip: In evaluating candidates, keep market trends in mind. If shorter employment tenure and/or career and industry crossover is common and accepted in your industry, don't hold such experiences against a job candidate you're evaluating.

## Avoiding common mistakes

Even though you may take a structured, methodical approach to evaluating the interviewees, the evaluation process will still have a subjective component. And whenever people use subjective judgment processes, biases can creep in. Being aware of the following common mistakes can help you remain as neutral as possible:

- Being overly impressed with maturity or experience, or overly dismayed by youth and immaturity

- Mistaking a quiet, reserved, or calm demeanor for lack of motivation

- Mistaking the person's ability to play "the interview game," or his or her ability to talk easily, for intelligence or competence

- Allowing personal biases to influence your assessment; for example, you might be tempted to judge the candidate harshly or discredit the opinions of your team members because the candidate reminds you of someone you dislike

- Looking for a friend or for a reflection of yourself in the candidate

- Assuming that graduates of certain institutions or former employees of certain organizations are automatically best qualified

- Giving too much weight to a candidate's ability to speak the jargon of your business

- Focusing on one or two key strengths and overlooking the absence of other important qualities

- Failing to value motivation to get ahead

- Ignoring feedback from team members and looking at the candidate from your perspective only

- Weighing the impact this person will have on *your* position, such as improvements to processes that may affect your job

---

Tip: While evaluating candidates, don't focus solely on comparing them with each other. Also, compare each candidate with the high-performer candidate profile, and look for a match.

---

## Checking references

Reference checks verify claims made by the candidate during the interview process and fill in information gaps. They can also provide valuable outside perspectives on the candidate and his or her potential fit with the position.

Check references near the end of the interviewing process, when you are close to making a decision. If you have not already discussed reference checking with the candidates, be sure to obtain their permission to do so. Otherwise, you may jeopardize their current employment. For example, if you know someone who works at a candidate's current employer and phone the colleague to ask about the candidate's qualifications, word may get around prematurely at the company that the person is looking for another job.

Use the telephone or e-mail to check references. Don't check references via letter; you probably won't get much information. When checking references:

- Take a little time to build rapport with the reference.

- Briefly describe the job that the candidate is applying for.

- Beware of the legal ramifications of asking and answering inappropriate questions.

- Ask about the candidate's style, character, strengths, and weaknesses.

- Ask tough questions, and follow up with detailed probes.

The table "Sample questions to check references" provides a handy guide to this part of the interviewing process.

## Sample questions to check references

| Instead of asking . . . | Ask . . . |
| --- | --- |
| "Did Jack do a good job managing his department?" | "What was Jack best at?" |
| | "What did his subordinates like best about him?" |
| | "What did they like least?" |
| | "Are there any jobs that would be inappropriate for Jack?" |
| | "What kind of organizational environment would suit Jack best?" |

# Step 5: Making a Decision and a Job Offer

ONCE YOU'VE EVALUATED the candidates, it's time to make a decision and present a job offer. This choice can seem difficult, especially if you have the good fortune to have interviewed numerous promising candidates. The following recommendations can help you narrow the choices down and make an attractive job offer.

## Arriving at a choice

Résumés, interviews, and reference checks all inform the decision-making process. At some point, you must ask yourself, "Do we have sufficient information to make a decision?"

If the answer is yes, you are ready to make the hiring decision. Rank your top three candidates, make the offer to the top-ranked candidate, and prepare to be rejected by your first choice. You may have to make more than one job offer.

If the answer is "No, we have insufficient information," then ask yourself these questions:

- "What additional information do we need to make a decision?"

- "What uncertainties can we reasonably expect to reduce?"

- "Do the candidate's strengths outweigh his or her weaknesses?"

- "What can be taught on the job or developed with formal training?"

Handle the remaining uncertainties to the extent that time and cost constraints permit. For example, you may call some candidates back for another interview, or you may get several more team members involved in the interviewing process. Once you've taken these additional actions, move to a decision.

## Presenting an attractive job offer

Be sure you understand your organization's policy on who makes the job offer. In some organizations, the immediate supervisor or manager makes the offer. In others, the human resource department makes the offer.

Job offers are usually made in person or by telephone. In making an offer, be sure to:

- Express enthusiasm.

- Make the offer personal by referring to something positive that you recall about the interview.

- Continue to gather information from the candidate regarding any concerns he or she may have (such as the quality of career development opportunities at the company), the timing of the decision (is the person really ready to make the jump to a new job?), and other organizations he or she may be considering.

- Provide a time frame for the offer so that the candidate knows how much time he or she has to respond.

# What Would YOU Do?

## Toby, or Not Toby? That Is the Question.

J ACOB MANAGES ProCo's engineering team. The company has enjoyed steady growth, and Jacob needs to expand his team to help support that success. He creates a job profile describing the available position and advertises the opening. From the résumés he receives, he selects the most promising candidates and schedules interviews.

His first interviewee is Toby, a woman who currently works for a leading firm in ProCo's industry. She arrives on time and seems pleasant and intelligent, if a bit quiet. Jacob offers Toby a seat and chats casually for a few moments, to put her at ease. Jacob discovers that he and Toby grew up in adjacent towns. They talk about their hometowns briefly.

Jacob then wonders what he should say next to get the most from the interview. He thinks to himself, *Should I ask what class she was in, to put her further at ease? Should I try to gauge her attitude toward teamwork by asking her whether she believes she has a lot to offer our team?* He's just not sure how to move the interview forward so he can determine whether Toby is truly qualified for the job.

What would YOU do? The mentor will suggest a solution in *What You COULD Do.*

After extending a verbal offer, you should also send an offer letter. An offer letter is an official document, so be sure to seek advice from the appropriate sources (your company's HR and legal departments) before sending one. It is important to avoid implying that the offer is an employment contract, which is a document that stipulates matters such as how long the term of employment will be. An effective offer letter includes the following information:

- Starting date

- Job title

- Expected responsibilities

- Compensation

- Benefits summary

- Time limit for accepting the offer

The table "Sample offer letter," on the next page, shows how one company prepared an offer letter for a producer it wished to hire.

## Sample offer letter

November 1, 2008

Mr. Sunkiu Chang
<Home Address>

Dear Sunkiu:

It is my pleasure to formally offer you the position of producer at Cummins Industries. You will report to Sarah Jones, executive producer. Your base salary will be $1,500 semimonthly, which is equivalent to $36,000 annually. Your start date will be Monday, December 1. For a summary of your benefits, please see the attached folder of information.

Consistent with Cummins Industries' policy, the first three months of employment are an orientation and review period during which either the staff member or the employer may terminate employment if, for any reason, the placement is unsuitable.

Please indicate your acceptance of this offer by signing the enclosed copy of this letter and returning it and the enclosed forms to me within one week of this date.

I look forward to meeting you and having you join the staff at Cummins Industries. Please contact me if you have any questions about your new position.

Sincerely,

Carol Guglielmo
Vice President, Human Resources

AGREED AND ACCEPTED BY:

_____          _____

Sunkiu Chang                              Date


cc:  Martha Chisholm, President and CEO
     Sarah Jones, Executive Producer

# What You COULD Do.

### Remember Jacob's uncertainty about how to move forward in the interview with Toby?

Here's what the mentor suggests:

Jacob should *not* ask Toby what class she was in at Plainfield High. Because Jacob and Toby grew up in adjacent towns, it may seem natural for him to ask her this question—but doing so is actually illegal. In the United States, federal and state law prohibits asking questions that may reveal a candidate's age, such as when he or she graduated from high school or college.

Jacob should also avoid asking leading questions, such as "So, would you say you have a lot to offer this team?" This question would only direct Toby to answer with what Jacob wants to hear. Of course, Toby is going to say that she thinks she has a lot to offer Jacob's team. Leading questions won't help Jacob achieve his main objective in the interviewing process: to get as much information as possible from Toby so that he can make an informed choice.

His best bet would be to learn more about Toby's work experience—for example, by asking, "In what ways did you contribute to your team's effort in your last position?" Such accomplishment-related questions will help get Toby talking. They also will provide evidence of her demonstrated behavioral qualities. Her answers will reveal why and how she accomplished something she considers important and will suggest her level of involvement in the accomplishment.

# Tips and Tools

# Tools for
# Hiring an Employee

## Interview Preparation Form

*Use this form to prepare for a hiring interview, review the job profile, and make a list of the key responsibilities and tasks of the job, associated training and/or experience, and personal attributes required to do the job well. For each of the areas you need to explore with the candidate, prepare several questions in advance. After the interview, rate the candidate in each of the key areas on the Decision-Making Matrix.*

Job Title:

| Key Responsibilities and Tasks | Associated Training and/or Experience |
|---|---|
| 1. _____ | 1. _____ |
| 2. _____ | 2. _____ |
| 3. _____ | 3. _____ |
| 4. _____ | 4. _____ |

Personal Attributes to Look for:

| Key Areas to Explore | Questions to Ask | Notes |
|---|---|---|
| Education | 1. _____ | _____ |
| | 2. _____ | _____ |
| | 3. _____ | _____ |
| Previous Experience | 1. _____ | _____ |
| | 2. _____ | _____ |
| | 3. _____ | _____ |

| Key Areas to Explore | Questions to Ask | Notes |
|---|---|---|
| Job Accomplishments | 1. _____ <br> 2. _____ <br> 3. _____ | _____ <br> _____ <br> _____ |
| Skills and Knowledge | 1. _____ <br> 2. _____ <br> 3. _____ | _____ <br> _____ <br> _____ |
| Personal Attributes | 1. _____ <br> 2. _____ <br> 3. _____ | _____ <br> _____ <br> _____ |
| Previous Appraisal or Rating | 1. _____ <br> 2. _____ <br> 3. _____ | _____ <br> _____ <br> _____ |

## *Decision-Making Matrix*

*Use this worksheet to evaluate each job candidate for a particular position. Enter a score for each of the key areas. By tallying the total scores and reviewing your interview notes, you can begin to identify which candidate is the right person for the job.*

Job Title:

| Candidate Name | Key Area Ratings (poor) 1 to 5 (excellent) | | | | | | TOTAL |
| | Education | Previous Experience | Job Accomplishments | Skills and Knowledge | Personal Attributes | Previous Appraisal or Rating | |
|---|---|---|---|---|---|---|---|
| | | | | | | | |
| Notes: | | | | | | | |
| | | | | | | | |
| Notes: | | | | | | | |
| | | | | | | | |
| Notes: | | | | | | | |
| | | | | | | | |
| Notes: | | | | | | | |
| | | | | | | | |
| Notes: | | | | | | | |

# Job Description Form

*Complete this form before you begin interviewing candidates for an open position.*

Job Title: _____

Organization: _____

Hiring Manager: _____

Reporting Manager: _____

| Compensation: | Hours: | Location: |
|---|---|---|

### Job Summary



### Education Requirements



### Experience Requirements



### Personal Qualities Required



### Skill and Knowledge Requirements

1. _____
2. _____
3. _____
4. _____
5. _____
6. _____

### Job Responsibilities and Tasks

1. _____
2. _____
3. _____
4. _____
5. _____
6. _____
7. _____
8. _____
9. _____
10. _____

# Test Yourself

This section offers ten multiple-choice questions to help you identify your baseline knowledge of the essentials of hiring an employee. Answers to the questions are given at the end of the test.

**1.** When defining job requirements, you consider four areas. Three of these areas are primary responsibilities and tasks, background characteristics, and personal characteristics. What is the fourth area you should consider?

    a. Organizational structure and culture.

    b. The amount of compensation available for the position.

    c. The hiring and reporting manager.

**2.** Once you understand a position's requirements, the next step is to create a job description. What is the purpose of a job description?

    a. A job description enables you to see how your organization defines a particular job in comparison to how other organizations define the same or a similar position.

    b. A job description provides you with a way to evaluate candidates and quickly eliminate those who are unqualified.

    c. A job description allows you to explain the job to potential candidates and to resources you may be using to help you identify candidates.

**3.** What is the first step to take when you begin screening résumés?

  a. Eliminate the candidates who do not meet the basic education and experience requirements.

  b. Eliminate the candidates who work outside the industry.

  c. Determine whether you know any of the candidates.

**4.** What is the advantage of having an interview team?

  a. The interview process is less time-consuming because several people will be sharing the task.

  b. Each team member brings different experiences and perspectives to the process.

  c. The hiring decision can be made more quickly because the team members can use majority rule to select the best candidate.

**5.** You've decided to conduct initial in-person interviews. How many candidates might you want to meet, and how much time should you allot for each interview?

  a. Narrow the field to two to four candidates, and keep initial interviews to fifteen minutes.

  b. Narrow the field to four to seven candidates, and schedule thirty to sixty minutes per interview.

  c. Narrow the field to no more than a dozen candidates, and schedule thirty minutes for each interview.

**6.** Which type of interview is usually most effective?

    a. A structured interview in which all candidates answer the same set of questions.

    b. An unstructured interview in which you have unique conversations with each candidate based on his or her individual skills and experience.

    c. An interview that combines elements of a structured and an unstructured interview.

**7.** Which question is illegal to ask during a job interview?

    a. "Do you have any health-related issues that would prohibit you from doing this job?"

    b. "If hired, can you show proof that you are at least eighteen years of age?"

    c. "If hired, can you show proof of your eligibility to work in the United States?"

**8.** When you are evaluating candidates, which of the following is important to do?

    a. Finding a candidate who is likely to be compatible with your organizational culture and management style.

    b. Finding a candidate who is similar to you so you can be assured you will work well together.

    c. Finding a candidate who has worked for a direct competitor of your organization.

**9.** You are on the telephone with a candidate's reference. You hope to confirm your positive impressions, verify claims the candidate has made, and fill in any information gaps you may have. Which question is probably *not* going to give you useful information?

a. "What are her strengths and weaknesses?"

b. "What did her direct reports like best about her? What did they like least?"

c. "Did she do an effective job managing her department?"

**10.** What is the purpose of an offer letter?

a. An offer letter is used to make the initial job offer to the selected candidate.

b. An offer letter is sent to the candidate after the initial offer is made by phone to summarize the terms of the offer.

c. An offer letter is an employment contract that outlines the terms of the offer and that the candidate needs to sign and return to you to accept the position.

## Answers to test questions

**1, a.** By considering organizational structure and culture in addition to responsibilities and background and personal characteristics, you can more easily determine the attributes a job candidate would need to fit in with the organization as a whole.

**2, c.** A job description allows you to provide a thorough and consistent explanation of the job requirements to both potential candidates and recruiting resources.

**3, a.** By eliminating candidates who don't meet basic education and experience requirements, you make the screening process manageable and ensure that the candidates you consider have the background characteristics required for the position.

**4, b.** The broader view of the candidate and position afforded by the team members' different perspectives is more likely to lead to a successful hiring decision.

**5, b.** Do your best to limit the field to four to seven candidates and allow up to an hour per interview. For less demanding positions, you may find out everything you need to know about the candidate in this interview. Otherwise, you may need to see the candidate again.

**6, c.** Structured interviews enable you to easily compare candidates. Unstructured interviews offer the advantage of enabling you to get to know each individual. It's best to combine these two approaches. Ask all candidates a core set of questions, but be flexible and inquire about unique, interesting information on their résumés so you can learn more about them.

**7, a.** This question is phrased in such a way that it violates the candidate's individual rights. It's critical that you frame such a question in terms of specific job requirements. Legal wording would be, "This job requires that you lift 50 pounds. Are you able to meet this requirement?" If you are not familiar with these laws and regulations, consult your human resource specialist or legal counsel prior to interviewing.

**8, a.** Compatibility with your organizational culture and management style is one important criterion to consider as you're evaluating candidates. Additional criteria include essential technical experience, ability to grow in the organization, and compatibility with the organization's reward system, among others. Mistakes to avoid include looking for candidates who are like you and assuming that candidates who have worked for certain organizations will be highly qualified for the job.

**9, c.** This question probably won't give you useful information because it requires a simple yes or no response. You want more detailed responses than that. References are likely to give you more useful, detailed information when you ask open-ended questions about a candidate's style, character, strengths, and weaknesses. Ask tough questions and follow up with detailed probes.

**10, b.** An offer letter is used as a follow-up measure after the initial offer is made by phone. It outlines the job responsibilities and terms of the offer but is not an employment contract.

# To Learn More

## Articles

Butler, Timothy, and James Waldroop. "Understanding 'People' People." *Harvard Business Review* OnPoint Enhanced Edition (June 2004).

Nearly all areas of business—not just sales and human resources—call for interpersonal savvy. Relational know-how comprises a greater variety of aptitudes than many executives think. Some people can "talk a dog off a meat truck," as the saying goes. Others are great at resolving interpersonal conflicts. Some have a knack for translating high-level concepts for the masses. And others thrive when they're managing a team. Because people do their best work when it most closely matches their interests, the authors contend, managers can increase productivity by taking into account employees' relational interests and skills when making personnel choices and project assignments. The authors identify four dimensions of relational work: influence, interpersonal facilitation, relational creativity, and team leadership; and they offer practical advice to managers, including how to gauge the relational skills of potential employees during interviews.

DeLong, Thomas J., and Vineeta Vijayaraghavan. "Let's Hear It for 'B' Players." *Harvard Business Review* OnPoint Enhanced Edition (June 2003).

In the much-heralded war for talent, it's hardly surprising that companies have invested a lot of time, money, and energy in hiring and retaining star performers. For most CEOs, recruiting stars is simply more fun; for one thing, the young A players they interview often remind them of themselves at the same age. For another, A players' brilliance and drive are infectious; you simply want to be in their company. But our understandable fascination with star performers can lure us into the dangerous trap of underestimating the vital importance of the supporting actors. It's true that A players can make enormous contributions to performance. Yet, as the authors have found, companies' long-term performance—even survival—depends far more on the unsung commitment and contributions of their B players. These capable, steady performers are the best supporting actors of the corporate world. They counterbalance the ambitions of the company's high-performing visionaries. Unfortunately, organizations rarely learn to value their B players in ways that are gratifying for either the company or these employees. This article will help you to rethink the role of your organization's B players.

Groysberg, Boris, Ashish Nanda, and Nitin Nohria. "The Risky Business of Hiring Stars." *Harvard Business Review* (May 2004).

With the battle for the best and brightest people heating up again, you're most likely to be out there looking for first-rate talent in the ranks of your competitors. Chances are, you're sold on the idea of recruiting from outside your organization—developing people within the firm takes time and money. But the authors, who have tracked the careers of high-flying CEOs, researchers, software developers, and leading professionals, argue that top performers quickly fade after leaving one company for another. After a "star" moves on, research shows, not only does his performance plunge, but so does the effectiveness of the group he joins—and the market value of his new company. The authors conclude that companies should focus on cultivating talent from within and do everything possible to retain the stars they create.

"The Manager's Guide to Hiring and Retention Collection." *Harvard Management Update Collection* (February 2001).

This *Harvard Management Update* resource collection contains twelve articles aimed at helping hiring managers identify and hire great candidates and retain talented employees.

Menkes, Justin. "Hiring for Smarts." *Harvard Business Review* (November 2005).

Despite its shortcomings, the standard IQ test is still a better predictor of managerial success than any other assessment tool companies currently use, Justin Menkes argues. The author defines the specific subjects that make up "executive intelligence"—namely, accomplishing tasks, working with people, and judging oneself. He describes how to formulate questions to test job candidates for their mastery of these subjects, offering several examples based on real situations. The questions in an executive intelligence test shouldn't require specific industry expertise or experience; any knowledge they call for must be rudimentary and common to all executives. And the questions should not be designed to ask whether the candidate has a particular skill; they should be configured so that the candidate will have to demonstrate that skill in the course of answering them.

Morgan, Nick. "A Question of Survival." *Harvard Management Communication Letter* (August 2002).

Job interviews are always stressful, but at least most people know their way around the traditional questions—"Where do you see yourself in five years?" and the like. But many interviewers have tougher questions in store, and fielding them with aplomb can make the difference between being hired and being an also-ran. This article assesses some of the trickier questions and offers tips on how best to prepare for them.

Ross, Judith A. "Hiring for Intangibles." *Harvard Management Update* (January 2007).

Whether you're trying to fill an executive-level position or one closer to the front lines, intangibles such as attitude can spell the difference between a hire who proves merely competent and one who goes on to shine. How do you identify the intangibles you need—for example, creative problem solving, calm in the face of fire, teamwork, or doggedness—and then, how do you determine whether the job candidate you are considering offers them? *HMU* talks with management consultant Laurence Haughton and several company executives for their suggestions on making the best hire you can.

## Books

Harvard Business School Publishing. *Harvard Business Review on Finding and Keeping the Best People*. Boston: Harvard Business School Press, 2001.

This collection of cutting-edge articles will help organizations understand how best to hire and retain their top employees in today's fiercely competitive job market. The articles provide the reader with perspectives on not only how to hire and retain people, but also why employees leave and how to utilize their skills even after they're gone. Articles include "Toward a Career-Resilient Workforce" by Robert H. Waterman Jr., Judith A. Waterman, and Betsy A. Collard; "A Market-Driven Approach to Retaining Talent" by Peter Cappelli; "Hiring Without Firing" by Claudio Fernandez-Araoz; "Making Partner: A Mentor's Guide to the Psychological Journey" by Herminia Ibarra; "Who Wants to Manage a Millionaire?" by Suzy Wetlaufer; "Too Old to Learn?" by Diane Coutu; "Managing Away Bad Habits" by James Waldroop and Timothy Butler; and "Job Sculpting: The Art of Retaining Your Best People" by Timothy Butler and James Waldroop.

Harvard Business School Publishing. *Harvard Business Essentials Guide to Hiring and Keeping the Best People*. Boston: Harvard Business School Press, 2004.

> In today's ever-changing business environment, hiring an all-star workforce and keeping it in place is a challenge for any organization. With an overview on topics such as recruiting the right people, cultivating the right culture, avoiding employee burnout, and calculating employee turnover, *Hiring and Keeping the Best People* offers managers a clear understanding of how to hire more effectively and increase retention. Packed with hands-on tips and tools, this helpful guide provides actionable and practical advice for managers and human resource professionals alike.

## eLearning Programs

Harvard ManageMentor. *Hiring*. Boston: Harvard Business School Publishing, 2007.

> This interactive module sheds additional light on how to effectively manage every step in the hiring process. Concepts are augmented with hands-on activities, personal insights from leading experts in the business arena, and minicases that challenge you to apply your knowledge. A "Check Your Learning" test provides feedback on correct and incorrect answer choices.

# Sources for
# Hiring an Employee

The following sources aided in development of this topic:

Adams, Bob, and Peter Veruki. *Streetwise Hiring of Top Performers*. Holbrook, MA: Adams Media Corporation, 1997.

Harvard Business School, Human Resources. "Interviewing Skills," 1998.

Harvard Business School Publishing. *Hiring and Keeping the Best People*. Boston: Harvard Business School Press, 2002.

Harvard University, Office of the General Counsel. "Legal Issues in Hiring," (December 1997).

Hattersley, Michael. "Conducting a Great Job Interview." *Harvard Management Update* (March 1997).

Jenks, James M., and Brian L. P. Zevnik. "ABCs of Job Interviewing." *Harvard Business Review* (July–August 1989).

Kanter, Arnold B. *The Essential Book of Interviewing*. New York: Random House, 1995.

Roberts, Michael J. "Note on the Hiring and Selection Process." *Harvard Business School Case Note*, 1993.

Swan, William S. *How to Pick the Right People Program*. New York: John Wiley & Sons, 1989.

# Notes

# Notes

# Notes

# Notes

# Notes

# How to Order

Harvard Business Press publications are available worldwide from your local bookseller or online retailer.

You can also call:
1-800-668-6780

Our product consultants are available to help you 8:00 a.m.–6:00 p.m., Monday–Friday, Eastern Time. Outside the U.S. and Canada, call: 617-783-7450.

Please call about special discounts for quantities greater than ten.

You can order online at:
www.HBSPress.org